W9-DAF-184

LAST
HARVEST

Poems of
Bernard Grebanier

Library of Congress Catalog Card Number 79-87784
Copyright © 1980 by the Estate of Bernard Grebanier
All Rights Reserved
Printed in the United States of America
First Edition

FOR
LINCOLN BARROS
*who taught me fairly late in life that
there is no possession more precious or
more highly to be prized than that innate,
unconscious and unselfish goodness which
is his.*

CONTENTS

Editors' Note

This volume is our response to a request made by Bernard Grebanier in his Will that we arrange for the publication of those of his poems that were unpublished at the time of his death.

A portion of *The Trial* was published in *Motive* but the poem is published for the first time in its entirety here.

Where Bernard indicated the date on which a poem was written, we give that date.

Bernard put everything of himself into whatever task he was undertaking. Certainly the comments on poetry that appear throughout his *Enjoyment of Literature* (published earlier as Bernard's Introduction to the textbook which he prepared with Seymour Reiter, *Introduction to Imaginative Literature*) represent the full yield of a lifetime of critical thought regarding poetry. To look over this book for certain of Bernard's observations on poetry is to be once again stunned by the range here: the world of learning, the sense of civilization, the vitality, the immediacy, the capacity for significant distinction, the abundant humor, the incomparable grace. Who but Bernard Grebanier would demonstrate the difference between what is and what is not poetry by taking a bit from Barron's National Financial Weekly which opens with the deathless words:

> Any day now, the dredges and tugs of the Great
> Lakes Dredge & Dock Co. of Chicago . . .

and first splitting the passage up into lines, then into pentameter, then turning it into an ode, in an effort to see whether in any of these manifestations the words become poetry, leaving fixed in the reader's mind as no other device

1

could possibly do just why it is that they remain inalterably prose?

The following section from *Enjoyment of Literature* is typical of what Bernard Grebanier had to bring to a discussion of poetry:

Poetry thus is a more condensed, more vivid, more intense medium of expression than prose. Prose cannot entirely dispense with the language of ideas, which is abstract, no matter how rich in imagery any given passage may be. Strictly speaking, in prose images are, as we have already said, less generic than in poetry. "With most poets," we have remarked, "imagery has been the lifeblood of their poetry .... While in prose the image is often the riveter of our attention or the welcome oasis in the desert—in poetry the image becomes the tissue itself of the poet's thought." We said this so long ago, that we are in hopes it will in this place have fresh meaning. Vice versa, abstractions are not generic to poetry, though a poet may introduce a philosophic idea nakedly:

> *Beauty is truth, truth beauty*
> —"Ode on a Grecian Urn" by KEATS

A poem is not necessarily better for the intrusion of such an abstraction, and some poets would certainly insist on conveying such an idea through imagery rather than permit themselves to state it so baldly. At any rate, if the rest of Keats's ode were written in that kind of language, it would not be a poem at all. The "Ode on a Grecian Urn" contains, except for its conclusion, a series of magnificent images; the poet, therefore, may be permitted his moment of prose, which is affixed as a sort of motto at the conclusion.

It is the fact that poetry lives by the image that distinguishes it from prose. And that is its advantage. That is what enables a poet to say far more in a few lines than prose could say in a page, and yet leave still more implied. In prose, a pessimistic philosopher might say:

Life has no meaning. Regarded superficially, it gives the illusion of significance. We exert ourselves, we become involved in all sorts of plans, activities, hopes, ambitions. But when the totality of these endeavors is examined, we can discern in them no recognizable design, no goal achieved, no purpose uniting the whole. All our anguish, despair, joy, ecstasy, rebellion are without import.

2

He might multiply his words many times over, but he could never manage to say more in this strain than Macbeth does in a few words (V/v/27 seq.):

> *It is a tale*
> *Told by an idiot, full of sound and fury,*
> *Signifying nothing.*

One brilliant image of a poem says more than a paragraph of prose.

This intensity of meaning conveyed by the language of imagery, since imagery is fundamental to poetry, is the chief distinguishing trait of poetry. But there are other differences from prose.

Words when spoken make sound, and there are therefore inevitably certain musical attributes which attach to language. Writing in prose or verse, the author has available to him a variety of these musical attributes, which become part of his meaning too. In poetry these musical attributes are relatively more formal and at the same time more basic than in prose. Rhythm, for instance, is based on firmer patterns in poetry than in prose. Rhyme, which can be a source of much power and beauty in poetry, has almost no place in prose at all. Musical attributes, then, are by the differences in their uses in poetry and prose a further cause of differences between the two media.

As his many friends know, Bernard lived for perhaps thirty years on a fourth-floor apartment overlooking Broadway on the West Side of New York City. No man ever had a more highly developed sense of civilization, past and present, than did Bernard Grebanier. In recent times the civilization that Bernard revered was in low ebb—Bernard had no illusions about this. The signs of this low ebb were apparent on Bernard's Broadway as they were elsewhere in our society. As one walked on Broadway, one encountered much that seemed ugly and dark. Yet, when one reached 88th Street, if one looked up to the windows of the corner apartment on the northeast side, one saw the light on, and one took heart: Bernard Grebanier was at work. The Lord only knows what the work might be. He might very well be writing poems—some of the poems that appear here. He might be writing prose—fiction or nonfiction. He might be teaching—Shakespeare to those students who could never allow him to cease teaching Shakespeare, or the piano. He might be playing the piano or the harpsichord. He might be cooking dinner by himself for a party of twelve. Whatever his work was, one knew that it would be executed with authority and deftness and penetration and wit and passion and subtlety and incomparable grace. One knew that all was not dark. The light was on. Bernard Grebanier was at work.

It is inconceivable that he is not with us.

What Chesterton said of Shaw is equally true for Bernard:

But this shall be written of our time: that when the spirit who denies besieged the last citadel, blaspheming life itself, there were some, there was one especially, whose voice was heard and whose spear was never broken.

Richard Matthews
Philip Winsor

SHORTER
POEMS

THE PARAMECIA

The paramecia, in slipper shod
Among their fellow-protograms swarm;
Amoebae, unprepossessing, on their quod
Still show the eye a clear, if spreading, form.
The shrimp, the gastropod and microcyte,
The dinosaur, the weasel, pygmy, elf,
Gorilla, rhino, each pre-Adamite
Had shape identifying self—
Its line, configuration, which constrained
The viewer well to note a contour unique.
But these "creators" of our time have strained
To turn Life back to Chaos, form to freak.
Nature's Law, perceived sense unprofaned,
Decrees that Life in form *must be contained*.

ARTISTS AND ACADEMIES

Academies, once formed, have quick acclaimed
The poet—*if* his works are à la mode—
And new one's lucubrations yearly named
As genius. Obscenities? He's on the road
Where only thousand thousands "dare to tread"—
Is truly "of his times." Now he enjoys
An eminence among us. He'll be read
Most while his poet's function he destroys
And while that fashion lasts—but that's not long;
For he forgets "awards" will never keep
Him in the company of those whose song
Is deathless, despite the plaudits he may reap.
 Poor luminary all the roars enjoys.
 But stars of heaven do not make a noise.

VALEDICTORY TO LOVE

SONNET I
Meeting

You say that as I entered in that room,
My cloak cast loose, all others there were banished
By magic, as though relentless toll of doom
With one clear clang your past and mine had vanished.
I saw you from the corner of my eye,
Not catching yours, which followed where my way
Might lead me (you confess). "I don't know why,"
I thought, "But there's a friend I must waylay."
In but a moment you had settled all:
You crossed the space between us, made it plain
Whatever chance should from that hour befall,
The two of us should never more be twain.
  If so, you now belong to me, and I
  Belong to you until the day I die!

II
A Bow-Tie is Adjusted

They introduced us. First you bowed politely,
Then shyly searched for understanding, sought
Some sign (not there yet!), hint I might have caught,
Passion's sweet contagion; you leaned but slightly—
To match, you said, the collar's points more rightly
As your own elegance would pinch the knot—
My bow-tie was not fixed, you thought, quite taut.
With gossamer three fingers you set it brightly.
One touch? Too much! You snapped a joint upon
The silk, now satisfied. Though not your whim
To graze my skin with hand of yours, that care
Of tie beneath your eyes' commanding sun
Illumed the darkness, turned to ash my limb—
And trapped my life in love's unyielding snare!

9

III
What Impulse Caused You

What impulse caused you wish to blaze your sun
On me, while I, concealed within the dark
With hope that callous Death who'd not spared one
Whom sole I loved, I praying he would mark
My brow as next his summons, waking morning
To find in stark despair that still I lived
To waste perforce the endless day's suborning
My tasks dispirited and sedatived?
Why did you wake to life a heart whose hope
Was swift oblivion? How dared you smite
My nerves to brave the labyrinth and grope
The tangled way I'd lost up to the light?
Abraided, torn, I've found my way above,
Led to safety by your hand of love.

MARIANA IN THE NORTH

("For men tweeds, as ever, will be appropriate"—fashion note)

Make love to me in tweeds!
Let others pant in gabardine
Or broadcloth—and provoke my spleen;
    To such no heart accedes.

O come to me in tweeds!
If Pyramus have tryst with Thisbe,
What other garb, think you, should his be
    As to his love he speeds?

Take leave of me in tweeds!
And make me dream of Scotland's lochs,
Of Eire's meads, and fleecy flocks
    That graze in peaceful Leeds.

Make love to me in tweeds!
Silk or satin, cloth-of-gold
Leave this maiden's passions cold;
Not alone the warrior bold
Is fit love's kingdom firm to hold:
It's he, as ever, fills love's needs
Who makes his love to me in tweeds!

TRIOLETS

FOR R and D

1-

Our love-feasts shall remain unknown;
   we meet for love like guilty thieves,
   nor let the world our love be shown—
   our love-feasts shall remain unknown,
   prevent malicious gossip blown
   for hypocrites to snatch the leaves.
Our love-feasts shall remain unknown;
   we meet for love like guilty thieves.

2-

We meet for love like guilty thieves;
   but mutual love's without a taint;
   while light or rain falls on the leaves
   we meet for love like guilty thieves;
   like slyest babes on Christmas eves
   we kiss our gifts without restraint.
We meet for love like guilty thieves;
   but mutual love's without a taint.

HYMN TO ARTEMIS

a Pindaric Ode on the Inauguration of her Mysteries at Hope House,
September 1, 1952.

(Strophe)
Daughter of far-wandering and long-neglected
Leto, whom Thy sire Zeus, the Heavens' King,
Father of all gods and men, at length did bring
safe to Delos drifting on the tides, protected
his belovèd and those cherished two her womb
carried still concealed from Hera's hated eyes,
chaining fast the floating isle with adamant
firm to bottom of the sea, that earth might grant
shelter sought so long of her, and yield the room
where she might deliver to the light her prize—

(Antistrophe)
Thee and, brother of Thy bow, Apollo, both
born beside the sacred lake, which from that time
drew to worship by her bank from every clime
votaries of light, both his and Thine, not loth
venturing traverse the rugged mountain-height,
crossing churning oceans perilous to bark
stoutest timbered, but to bring Thee gifts of heart,
dauntless lovers of the chase who prayed their dart
sure and blameless Thou would'st bless in sun and night,
open field and forest, when it seek its mark.

(Epode)
Goddess mild and dread!—
tender of the doe,
nourishing the herd with herb and leaf,
melting with Thy fire what frost has frozen—
speeding yet unerringly the arrow
when the victim has been chosen—

13

who, when wroth, will harrow
multitudes with woe,
visiting upon them sudden death—
who could kiss the young Endymion in sleep
where he lay unknowing of Thy breath
light as music of Thy beams,
leaving undisturbed his dreams!
Goddess! Vain it were for us to sail the deep
seeking Delos for Thy sake!
From Thy sacred site the waters of Thy lake
are fled,
are dead,
as my eyes beheld but late with grief!
Where the holy temples once did stand
midst the shrubs and soaring cypress overgrown with vine,
lie but broken stone and arid sand
which but prickly nettles now their stunted lives entwine!
Here, hard by where tranquil waters stream,
which oft Thy light paves wide with silvered gleam,—
here within this verdant park
trimmed with curving aisles of box
decorous with many flowering trees
(handiwork of her who long
served Thee well with song,
chiming pack and leaping steed,
following where Thou didst lead
often ere the Dawn usurped the dark
with her rosy locks
on dim horizon spread!),
here we bend to Thee our knees,
asking that Thy smile propitious shine
as we here establish this Thy shrine,
making this henceforth forevermore Thy sacred day
men shall hold in reverence when others pass away!

B.D.N.G.
for Althea Urn.

THE CARYATIDS OF THE ERECTHEUM

The moon is wan tonight; the clear-obscure,
unerring, cunningly knows how to shade
time's ravages; in beauty you stand sure,
serenely fronting aeons, undismayed,
brows lost in dark, erect in ageless pride
within the shadowed moonlight overhead.
Your lowered lids would sadly seem to chide
my well-meant sympathy, pale-spirited,
which swiftly simulated all that load
of massive stone you bear to the tragic role
which stricken Greece must play, while griefs corrode
her inner heart, annihilate her soul:
    "To live in pride," you say, "whatever chance may press,
      has ever been for Greece her chosen burden;
    to stand before the world unmoved beneath that stress
      in dignity, she holds sufficient guerdon!
                  (Athens, October 16, 1951)

LOVE: LIFE: DEATH

Love's lot's worse than death.
In death
There is no breath,
The pulse drops,
The heart stops;
Into a dreamless peace
All time must cease.

Love draws life from pain,
A pain
Seeks peace in vain,
And each breath
A little death
Whose span would seem to be
Eternity

(Summer 1947)

IMPOSSIBLE RESOLUTION

Yes, I've resolved a thousand times
To cease lampooning with my rhymes:

My epigrams cause much debate
In quarters where I've garnered hate—

(Among the Comrades and their clowns
Who peddle various hand-me-downs)

Should I be killed with arguebus?
Or would a dagger make less fuss?

Would tempered poison do the trick?
Or, better yet, a well-aimed brick?

I've sworn an oath to sting no more!
I'll patiently embrace each bore,

And greet with glee each platitude
Or keep, at least, my lips firm glued.

But now a new fool must appear
His dullness sticking out at ear!

I cannot put up with this ass!
I'll show his folly in a glass—
Whatever vengeance come to pass!

INTEGRITY

When I have scattered of my best abroad,
   too often have they crowned my head with bays—
   my acts were tarnished by men's praise.

When I have wished to labor valiantly,
   my footsteps found paths easy to ascend—
   too soon my task achieved its end.

When I have worked good deeds in secrecy,
   the goodness I aspired failed, for pride
   was often smirking at my side.

It's only when I find my thoughts are Yours
   and all my heart to You is lifted up
   that I become a glowing cup.

There's no completeness but in love of You,
   in that alone can failure have no part,
   since You can penetrate the heart.

THE BASIL AND THE MINT,

a poem for Christmas

Now Mary flees from Herod's wrath,
    the infant Jesus at her breast;
through farmer's fields she makes her path
    and seeks to find a place of rest.

She sees a farmer sowing seed
    and cries to him, "Dear plowman, go
and fetch your family with speed
    to lend their hands this field to mow."

"You mock," says he, "for you may see
    I'm only planting now the grain!"
"Yet go," she says. Unwillingly
    he runs up to his house again.

They hurry back. Where seed was sown
    the corn is ripe among its leaves.
He stops not till the field is mown
    and till his sons have bound the sheaves.

And Mary hides among the ears,
    her babe clasped tight within her arms.
And soon the stamp of steeds she hears
    and Herod come to do her harm.

"The woman with the child you've seen?"
    "I saw there both upon a morn.
But see, O King, the harvest's in—
    and that was when I sowed the corn."

The basil standing by perceived
  a corner of her robe is seen,
and winds its tendrils interleaved
  and covers her with all its green.

The mint nearby then murmurs low:
  "beneath the sheaves! You'll find her there!"
But Herod hears not, shouts to go,
  and leads his men to seek elsewhere.

Since then the basil blooms with fruit
  and maidens pluck its spicy dower.
The mint is cursed, and on its shoot
  the branches bear a seedless flower.

(Aug. 7, 1956)
[publ. Jan. 1957 *Catholic World*]

(EDITORS' NOTE: *this is Bernard's commentary (page 255 of* ENJOYMENT OF LITERATURE) *on the Mason sonnet:*

The American poet Madeline Mason (1913–   ), in her volume, *At the Ninth Hour: A Sonnet Sequence in a New Form* (1958), introduced what is now known as the Mason sonnet, an innovation that has inspired a number of fine poets to employ it in their poems. The rhyme scheme is *abc abc cbd badda*. The rhyme scheme does *not* imply that the sonnet is written in three pairs of three lines and a concluding passage of five. The charms of the Mason sonnet will be found in the harmonious design into which the sequence of repeated rhymes falls, as well as in the recurrence of the opening rhyme in the last line.

THREE MASON SONNETS

TO MADELINE MASON:
An Acrostic

Madeline, you've given the sonnet's line
A newer grace and an enchanting form
Diverting rhymes molded rigid by time,
Enabling poets all anew to shine
Like suns, or else like eager bees upswarm
In gathering fresh honey: your new rhyme
New fragrance offers, like blooms in summer's clime.
Even when passion's blights raise lightning storm,
Marauding stainless skies with sudden cloud,
Madeline, your poems provide a norm,
Affording us a flowing, smoothly fine,
Such as your rhymes inspire! How richly proud
One gifted, like to you, and laurel-browed,
Now companied by poets sibylline!

June 1, 1972

21

FORGIVENESS FOR A TRAITOR

Tell not me how you deplore the blade
you thrust between my ribs so subtly fine,
nor seek extenuate the circumstance
with what "you'd heard" or "thought" or "were afraid
that my great kindness might be a line"
to tangle you in gratitude, mischance
you into cabals' counterplots. No dance
of expiation, please, on knees, no brine
in eyes! Useless now apology!
Best save it for occasion when to mine
credulity may serve your masquerade—
as not your swift unmasked deceit with me!
Repentance has virtue when I safely see
it in the graveyard next those who have betrayed.

May 31, 1972

SPRING AFTERNOON

Mad!—with desk-tasks waiting for me still—
to stretch upon the grass in Maytime's light
without in cranium one thought profound!—
rather, busy tracing every frill
the filmy clouds are making in their flight.
I snatch a dandelion deep from the ground:
the cat-bird's call, unconvincing sound,
could tempt what dog? The cardinal's crest too bright
for sun, I edge between my teeth blade-grass;
　　a squirrel flees a hound in pretended fright;
　　two frantic sparrows decide to mock with will
　　a baptism in the dust. With sudden pass
　　a thrush soars up a gaping oak's crevasse,
　　demanding world's attention to his trill.

May 31, 1972.

THE
TRIAL

THE TRIAL

The atrium lay open to a sun
that baked the streets of old Jerusalem,
as Pontius Pilate, canopied in shade
beside his Claudia, turned from watching how
the silver fish were idling in and out
the pool's shifting fire-points, to where
the mottled marble of the courtyard quivered
beneath the blinding sunlight. He sighed, "Those stones
might serve the Jews as ovens for that harsh
unleavened bread they'll feel obliged to eat   10
this week of Passover." She smiled but kept
her gaze upon the waters at her feet.
"I thank the gods," he mused, "that for this feast
we'll have a week's release from their demands,
contentions, unceasing wailings, their complaints
and all their muddled religious bickering.
It seems this single god of theirs forbids
their entering the pretorium these days
lest so they should defile themselves. Defile!
This coarse, ungracious people, madmen all,   20
detesting Rome, too weak to battle us
as did the Gaul barbarians with arms,
yet thwarting us with insolence and rancor
at every turn—who more defiles the air?—
their feuding Pharisees and Sadducees!—
their zest for finding crimes amongst themselves
whose nature mind of man cannot discern,
and then in droves they're pulling at my toga
demanding Rome a death for some poor wretch—
Rome must be their arbiter—Rome,   30
whose power they mock with feigned servility

while stubbornly refusing to join our ranks
in military service—Rome, whose peace
they ever will abjure!"
"Dear Pilate, why
this blistering day do you incense yourself
like one of these same Jews?" his Claudia asked;
she lightly tapped his arm with jeweled hand,
and smiled, but did not meet his worried glance,
"when they're not here to grieve you must your thoughts   40
dwell on them?" Pilate groaned. "This exile I
endure for Rome, although small thanks I reap—
do they not pour their hate and calumny
into the Emperor's own ear in Rome
while here they fawn on me?—I could endure
if Rome ordained my exile anywhere
but here!" She laughed now joylessly, but saw
his frown and sadly spoke: "Forgive my words,
but truth to say, the Jews have little cause
to study your delight or ease, my lord—."   50
The rapid slap of sandals on the pavement,
each step escaping touch with heated stone,
announced the boy's delayed appearance with
the chalices of chilled wine, and not
till Pilate saw with softened look the lad
had shot across the beaming squares into
the house, Judea's Procurator spoke,
and then in milder tone. "Dear wife, you talk
(why should you not?) with woman's mind and heart   60
of matters foreign to your gentle thoughts.
What foreign more, beloved, who should grace
some rose-garden by our Tiber, than
your beauty planted in this mountain-desert?
You blame me in your heart that I removed
that time our arms from out Caesarea
into Jerusalem. You deem that so
I sought their fury. What I dared to risk
was risked for Rome. If those who held my place

26

before me feared to fix the seat of her
authority within this town revered
in Jewish superstition, I for one
could hold it only base that Rome avoid
to claim without their leave what is her own."

"You proved, my lord, that those were more discreet
who held the place before you." Anger died
in Pilate's countenance, his lids half closed.
"Discreeter? I was young in service then
among these lunatics. Who could have guessed
the lengths their rage would urge them? Down they rushed
in hordes to scream vituperations, down
to Caesarea. For hours I could not see
what dread abomination we had thrown
upon their Holy City. The crime when I
unwound the theme from their cacophony
of accusation? I perceived the crime
reposed in the image of the Emperor
our standards bear. Their god allows them not
one image—even not the Emperor's!"
He seized the goblet eagerly, drank wine
to drown (this Claudia knew) the memory
of slaughtered bodies of petitioners
whose protests Pilate vainly thought to quell
with blades of the centurions until
it seemed that all the Holy City would
submit to death before they should repeal
their threats, or cease to batter Roman guards
with staves and stones, and desecrate the form
offending on the banners. Harder to
forget that in the end perforce he had
recalled the Roman arms and standards. "Dear,"
his lady said, "your loyalty to Rome
is to commend—yet sure it was but folly
to think the Jews would change their sacred laws.
You were not ignorant—all Italy

well knows that prohibition; often we
heard young Alcinous, the sculptor, tell
in Mantua how he was cast by his
own kin and warned this native town of his
no more to visit once he caught the love   110
of stone in Athens from the carvers there.
You often heard of this, yet after you
were begged that you withdraw the ensigns home,
you would not yield, but soon within this house,
this very house that Herod built, anew
you sought their fury—made their priests to know
that here you hung the table votive to
the Emperor. Once more their wrath upsurged,
once more you would not bend until their plea
had moved Tiberius; the Emperor   120
himself rebuked you, and the tablets were
decreed the journey to Caesarea."

According, Pilate nodded wearily.
"Because I understand no creed, no act
of theirs, I never can accept like you—
and Italy!—their stubborn wilfulness.
The event, if it had proved I erred, had proved
that Rome is but a pyramid of error."
He caught the pity in the look wherewith
Claudia studied him, but then he knew   130
how far her thoughts, nor could he trace their road.
For now she slowly rose to sit beside
the pool's enbankment, bending low her face
as though to meet her image in the water.
He started as in long-drawn breath she spoke:
"Be Rome a pyramid of right or wrong,
does it repose upon your shoulders—or
on theirs? Alas! you'd be now more than I
far happier by Tiber! I these nights,
on many a night, have dreamed such dreams, my lord,   140
have dreamed such dreams as fill my days with dread!

In wrath you blame the Jews for choosing peace
and scorn them that they do not threaten arms.
Do you forget: for Judas Maccabeus
they drained their veins of seas of blood that he
might sail in them to wrest from Syria
the liberty they cherished? We know well—
yes, many live who yet recall the time—
how John Hyrcanus and Aristobulus
his son smote fear into Judea's foes,   150
victorious in many bloody fields.
And we know well that had not civil broils
that followed in the savage fight between
the ambitious sons of Alexander, left
Judea prey to Pompey's strategy,
this land would still be free of Rome—and you!"
His stifled muttering awoke compunction
for Pilate's pride, yet she refrained from turning
but spoke as though her auditor were that
grave countenance reflected in the pool.   160
"I ask your pardon that my words should pain
your ears, but I should love you less could I
withhold from you my dread. My dreams presage
some scatheful act compacted in this town
disasterous to your life; and while contempt
and loathing for the Jews so rule your deeds
you daily figure as their enemy
who, did you will to be, might stand their friend.
My lord, beloved lord, I fear!" And now
she raised toward him a visage terror-torn   170
and forth her eyes such fears as caused him cry:
"My love! What dreams so fierce are these to dark
your face like one come back from Tartarus to earth!"
With care he hurried to her side,
but ere his hands could comfort her, she rose,
her eyes wide-opened, rapt, and held him off,
while granite-like she stood, her jewels sparkling
in sun. "To Tartarus this night I've been—

29

and saw you there—and saw—!" But here the words
were strangled in her throat, and she could say
no more. One moment something of her fright
infected him, but soon himself recalled
he roughly seized her arms and sternly spoke:
"Are you indeed that Claudia Procula,
descended of the Claudia Gens whose line
is pointed at in Rome for stubborn pride
and—yes! for cold disdain and arrogance?
And can a foolish dream, a tortured scene
Jerusalem's parched clime has burned upon
your fancy, lose you from your reason? This   190
by much I count the gravest wrong the Jews
afflict me with, that Claudia can forget
herself and fall their prey!" With quiet hand
he led her back beneath the canopy;
when he beheld her shaken less, he murmured:
"I ask what you would have me do, good wife?
How shall I ease the horror in your heart?"
"I do not know," she breathed, "I only know
I fear." In sadness Pilate shook his head,
"My Claudia, it was an evil day   200
I begged the Emperor set aside the law
which had forbid my having you with me,
and moved him grant my life amidst these plagues
be lightened by your presence and our love.
He proved magnanimous to me, but you
too dearly pay my need. This land I hate—
I do confess I burn with hate of it!—
infested (like the vermin nowhere here
to be escaped) with madness, has deeply bitten
the bane into your blood. That you should cringe   210
at dreams! That you arraign me where your love
should grow in pride for all I hazarded!
Upon my twice-miscarried aim to place
the argent emblems of Tiberius
in honor, you heap blame—a riddle to

expound—from you my wife, of Claudian line!
Not till today has Claudia Procula
forced Pilate to beseech her commendation
for aught the Procurator acts. Such crumbs
it is not fit that Caesar's proxy play
the beggar to implore. This day you fail me!
My wife speaks nothing of the toil
wherewith I've hoped to lift these reptiles up
into the light: I found Jerusalem
a desert; these bath-detesting loons, for all
the turbulence they make of what must be
unclean or clean to please their god, did they
essay for centuries to make provision
for water—first of wants that nature asks
supplied? Not even water! Claudia,   230
it is not many months since I have tapped
for them those fine capacious reservoirs
near Bethlehem by aqueducts which proof
against the ravages of wind and rain
will stand a century of centuries
along its many miles!—achieved despite
their ill-divining auguries. What gift
of greater boon could I bestow than this
upon an arid land? And how they thanked!
Their priests, with access to the water stored
from rains, which underlies their Temple's plat,   240
who lacked no water for themselves, were wroth
though all the city benefited this,
and easily fomented fury midst
a rabble ever ready to be kindled,
and made my gift another outrage planned.
Tumultuous they crowded to this house
when once the work was done. A sacrilege!'
they whined. And had I not our men disguised
among their multitude to lay about
their swords, I'd had new carnage charged to me,   250
no doubt. A sacrilege to succor them!"

31

"It was a sacrilege, my lord," his wife
now calmer, murmured, "sacrilege to rob
their Temple's treasury to pay a gift
unasked." "Why not?" he cried, as sudden stung
to anger, from his soul there burst at last
the words to paint the years' confusion he
had staggered in since he had known Judea.
"Why should that hoarded sum have been untouched
for public use? Because it was their god's—   260
for so their wealthy Saducees denounced—?
What god? Who sees him ever? In what shape?"
"What shape holds Jove?" his lady asked. As though
at stranger Pilate lifted brow at her,
and echoed in amaze, "What shape holds Jove?
Within his multiplex own sanctuaries
you know his form, as who does not? Our gods
are evident as are the sun, the moon,
the stars; and as the moon, the stars, the sun,
they manifest themselves to all the world—   270
not only so, as well in every fact
diurnal or nocturnal, yours or mine.
When I to Jupiter make my devotion
upon the Ides, I come, if so I will,
to Heaven's Most High and Best, the Lord of Heaven,
there where upon our Capitolium
aloft the Rock Tarpeian stands his fane;
as fits the Prince of Light, his priests white-capped
receive the sacrificed white lambs from out
my hands as I stand robed in white, for Jove's   280
Quadriga's imaged there, the thunder's wain
that's charioted by four white horses. At
this shrine triumphal marches ever end
when generals in victory must place
upon the knees of Jupiter the wreath
of laurel and will make an offering
to him of whitest oxen as Invictus,
the Lord of Victories. Beside him sit

proud Fides, patroness of faith and honor,
and she, the conqueror's guide, Victoria,   290
companions both to Jove, who rules in all
affairs that traffic with earth's Justice, oaths
and faithfulness. Should weather threaten havoc
we seek him out in other guise: as lord
of rains, of storms and thunder, lightning—we
make prayer to Jupiter as Pluvius,
or Fulgurator, Fulminator, or
as Tonans. Rome's own lord, he's worshipped now
as Victor, Imperator, now as Stayer
of Flight, now as Praedatus; and his temples   300
and figure stand in Rome beheld and known
in every spot agreeing to the power
that title manifests. Not so with Jove
alone. The first of March you women pay
your Matronalian due to Juno, Queen
of Heaven, Queen of all created women.
By virgins she is named as Virginalis,
Matrona by the wedded. You worship her
as Juga, president of marriage. June
is consecrate to her and nuptial-rites.   310
In childbed you invoke her as Lucina;
the guardian, she, of money as Moneta,
her sanctuary on the Capitol.
The merchants, should they choose, can also pray
to Mercury, whose magic well the Gate
Capena shades, or seek him in the Circus
for there of old he has been honored. Trades
look to Minerva, and the arts as well;
it's she who grants men prudently endure,
or gives them heart, in battle, wisest goddess,   320
who guides in war, and shines in peace her wisdom;
it's she who first designed the instruments
of music; and therefore they're purified
on her Quinquatrus.—In the spring we think
of Venus Murcia, whose fragrant myrtle

33

we hold as sacred. To Venus Victrix who
can grant to lovers gift of victory
in love, I thought it wise to come when I
sought love of you, and in her radiant temple
(built in piety to her by Caesar)   330
I asked the Queen of Love to touch your heart."

Cool radiance that columned serpentine
partakes of setting sunrays flickered in
his eyes while Pilate, then oblivious of
Jerusalem, in fancy walked the ways
of Rome;—so well contented, although briefly,
his lady smiled in pity what her lips
derision-curled could not refrain to sigh:
"Your soul's so perfectly the Roman, love,
you take delight so honestly in shape   340
and harmony of many-colored marble,
I'm less than kind to ask that you essay
beneath the worthy citizen of Rome
to excavate and find how deep and true
foundations of your faith may lie at root.
You thought it wise to sue the goddess' aid—
that Venus Victrix for your sake subdue
my heart to you—if she (and I!) approved—
though wise, not needful, am I to infer?
Had you not sued to her? Dear Pilate, swear   350
an oath to Jupiter, the Arbiter
of oaths, that you're persuaded it's Love's Queen
who granted me to you, that Venus' help
unasked had found me wedded to that too!
my mother favored.—Ah, but then! what god
shall hold in pawn your oath to Jupiter?"
Displeasure reddened Pilate's face, his eyes
flashed sparks of anger. "What you speak I hear,
the words I know, but I am lost in their
intent. Say, do we dwell again in your   360
Tartarean dream or do you stigmatize

34

me impious, portray me perjuror
to Jupiter?"
              "Ah no! not impious,
and not perjurious, my love,"—she took
his hand and placed it on her heart, the while
her eyes gave warrant too she spoke in love—
"but only apathetic to your gods.
No, hearken to mé! Don't rehearse for me
your ceremonies done, your sacrifices
and votive offerings paid—." "In such affairs   370
does any Roman find me wanting in
my duties?" "None, I'll vow! There's none more mindful
of calendar of holy days than you;
no Roman, not the priests themselves could find
you failing in observance to the gods.
In such affairs (I seize your phrase, my lord)
you are deep beyond reproach. The service is
reciprocal between the gods, my dear, and you!
The gods have reared my Pilate to high station
and showered him with gifts, and Pilate's soul   380
is far too clear to nurse ingratitude.
He knows it wise to fail them in no thanks
in such affairs! The balance even poised,
the gods and he exchange their gifts with pleasure!"
Impetuously, his hand, which to her breast
she kept clasped close a prisoner, he freed,
for Pilate now was tossed from ire to the sense
his lady mocked him like a boy at school.
"If this, then, be the language that piety
employs, good Claudia, impious let me be!
By Hercules! You speak a stranger tongue!
We've been unparted many years, else I
should think you fallen to some mad exotic,
mysterious, new-fangled cult, import
of Egypt by our fashionable dames
at home, who, ever eager to benight
their heads with novelty, in vastest numbers

35

forsake our old Olympus. Worse, I feel
encased within the verbal shell of what
you say, fanaticism which my teeth
have ground against full often among these Jews!"
"Fanaticism, eagerness of faith
is indexed prime offense with you, my lord,
I think." She turned aside from him and faced
the sun, which lowering in the West would soon
behind that thin-spun cloud decline, and though
she marked not setting sun nor rosy hue
with which the western sky appeased the fires
it beamed, she shivered as if night were come,
but shivered at her thoughts, for night was there.   410
And Pilate, quenching pity or caress,
indulged no motion for her audience,
but gazed before him, and for ease he built
again in air the pillared walks of Rome
he loved of old to haunt, addressing them:
"Philosopher and sage exhort all things
be done in moderation, and my taste,
you have observed, is seemliness. It's true
the gods and our most holy Emperor
have been most gracious, though I'm scion of   420
a liberated slave (was that your hint,
my Claudia?); Pilate were but graceless should he
neglect the rites of Rome's divinities
or of the Emperor. These duties I've
intextured as a part of such a life
as I would live; decorum, decency
require as much. Tiberius and Heaven's
Commanders, kept propriate, exact
no more. Who holds in mind Rome's history
and ancient virtues, holds such faith as mine.   430
Who'd hold exceeding this, I name no Roman!
And it's their fever that I cannot fathom
in Jews. Religion here, indecorous,
becomes not piece of life, but life itself.
That time the emblems of Tiberius

provoked revolt within Jerusalem,
when I at first rejected their demands
and threatened death, they willingly made bare
their throats to naked swords, and welcomed death
before the fancied wrong to their lone god.   440
What Roman lives at odds like these with Heaven?
Our deities would have us live, not die;
or dying, die that glory and dominion
accrue to Rome, and tame abiding to
our sons and theirs, who own our name in trust
Between Jerusalem and Rome can not
be ever amity, I vouch, or peace.
Rome rules a world. Recite within that world
where we won't make with home divinities
some truce? Benevolently Rome withholds   450
its hand from strife against barbarian gods
and spares their temples. Roman peace, not proud
to bend, does not abstain interpreting
whom conquered peoples worship as our gods,
revealed to them by other titles, since
the sun, the moon, the stars shine everywhere,
the sea laps many shores, we share the Earth
in common parenthood—and where their gods
may prove exotic to old Roman use,
unlocks the portals of our pantheon   460
to make them room. We hold no altercation
with names or deities whose purport's clear.
The sun-god, sure, beams not irate if he
be hailed as Helios, Horus, Sol, Apollo—
whatever called, hears tranquilly his name.
In country fields where Faunus rules, the folk
as Pan, as Lupercus, as Inuus
pay service to him.—How with these will sit
this Jewish god, unseen, unlineaged,
intolerant divine society?   470
(Intolerant of men as well, indeed!)
Their tabulated prohibitions form
a scroll out-paging Homer, and I well

37

construe the comfortless existence forced
by him is what endears him to the Jews!)
Think what execrations if on fond
suggestion we invited their Jehovah
to join Olympus' confraternity!
Not satisfied to be their only god,
their Lord forbids them grant to other lands   480
their own divinities. I cannot bear
the arrogance these monotheists flaunt;
as though sound reason were not undermined
enough by unintelligible stuff
and trumpery unheard-of, such as their
religion sums, they'd have all deities
to abdicate their altars! All the peoples
must kneel before Jehovah only; Rome,
in sequence, humbly must submit to Jews
the sceptred power won by Roman blood!   490
No, no! I say no amity for us
and them! However weak they seem, the war's
to death between Judea and our Rome.
I prophesy we count us never safe
until this race is subjugate, until
Jerusalem is levelled stone by stone!"

The light fast faded. Pilate, vacant now
his wrath at last, glanced quick where all this space
his Claudia, sunset-charmed, not turned nor moved.
Soft rays made burnished all her heavy tresses;   500
the yellow sapphires on her arm diffused
soft liquid light. Then quietly she spoke
as to herself: "The sun sinks, the light
will go, the darkened lands must suffer night.
Jerusalem, though razed, shall fan such fire
from out its ashes as will make of Rome
and all that Rome has vanquished one consuming
vast conflagration, if my dreams say true."

"Your dreams!" her husband murmured. "What's a dream
that it prove false or true? And what is truth?"   510

38

BOOK ONE

The Adversaries

Now was the time for Jesus to come down
into Jerusalem, whose streets, thick-packed
with pilgrims there to see the Passover,
he knew must prove to him a den of wolves
and field of triumph.

        Six long moons since he
had quit beloved Galilee forever;
six moons since brothers, weak, malevolent,
had dared him brave the world with acts; six moons
since he had followed in their loveless steps
alone (alone, too, when disciples tended   10
and walked with him in love—and ignorance!),
alone into Jerusalem. But then
that Feast of Lights he taught within the Temple
and bade who thirsted drink from him the streams
of living water; many drank that day
and knew him as a prophet; none laid hands
on him, the ready stones uncast which fists
in anger clutched, and Jesus went unharmed.
But from the priests' arrest then Jesus, forced
to flee—for that was not his hour—trod   20
the dusty road to Jericho, and thence
cross Jordan (purlieus where once John had baptized
the unknown Master), there to linger while
great numbers came believing him, till word
was brought that Lazar, whom he loved, was ill,
and love directed him to Bethany,
hard by Jerusalem; where Martha at
their table served, while Judas groaned that nard
three hundred bright denarii in worth
was lavished on those weary feet in love.   30
Six days before the Passover, that was,
and on that Sabbath crowds up-poured from out

39

the town to visit Jesus and behold
his friend, live Lazar, risen from the dead.

Meanwhile, unmindful on its mighty hill
the Temple, fiery gold and blinding white,
its golden spike-points rearing sun-defiant,
plied busy trade. The Holy Ark, its long
and toilsome trackless pilgrimages past,
here on the Temple mount had come to rest,   40
while centuries that passed enclosed with stone,
with double stone and triple, till in stone
a citadel and fortress, bastioned, closed,
and towered, hid the Holiest of Holies.
Redoubtable, impregnable, the walls
(the spirit petrified like Herod's heart,
their latest builder) cased a superflux
of busy life, the coming and the going—
confluent, percolating, idling through
piazzas, terraces, and colonnades,   50
and stairways intricate with winding passage.
Bazaar and fortress, market place and bank,
the politician's, scholar's forum now,
with warehouse, strongbox, guardrooms—all for hire.
Gold and marble! Fiery gold and snow!
Effulgent gold ablaze of metal-plate
and snow of marble-fire that cold in sun
of noonday flashed!

           Another fire than gold's
had flashed that distant time on Sinai's mount
when like devouring fire Sinai burned   60
on eyes that searched the cloud whence spoke the Lord
with Moses! Far too long that time, too soon
forgot! Too long ago the pillared cloud
stood by the tabernacle door and Moses
beamed on his children there a rosy light!
Too long, it was, since drawn by sweating ox

40

across the parching desert, the Holy Ark,
aloof the blood poured for Jehovah's sake,
unconquerable had sought the holy soil!
To keep inviolate the double tables,   70
the covenant divinely autographed,
what sanguinary hazard, weary toil
God's chosen braved! How staunch their faith when boldly
the Levites marched through Jordan's torrent, bore
the Ark, the people following, and made
for Jericho, whose walls came sundering
at sounding blasts of seven trumps of ram
before the Ark at Joshua's command!
And God delivered them to Joshua
and gave to Israel a land for which   80
they had not labored, oliveyards and vines
they had not planted, cities other hands
had built.

        Few years, and Israel, declined,
in folly fetched the sacred Ark in hopes
that it would guide at Ebenezer war
against the Philistines; unwilling that
such superstition shield their evil deeds
(for Eli's sons had wickedly profaned
the Ark—its door had seen vile doings done)
as though possession of the tables should   90
relax, not make intenser, moral law,
the Lord rebuked their madness, and withdrew
His glory out of Israel that day,
permitted capture of His covenant
by Philistines, who brought the captive Ark
to Dagon's house at Ashdod. But the Lord
took long to tire of His ingrate people,
nor granted long rejoicing to their foes;
in fear the Philistines beheld their god
cast down decapitate and armless prone.   100
So heavy fell the hand of God that cries
of anguish sounded through Philistia's streets.

41

Their eagerness to seize was less than to
release that prisoner! They heaped up jewels
upon the cart they drove to Bethshemeth
when they brought back the Ark to Israel!
Then glad enough the men came rushing down
from Kirjath-jearim to bring it home!

At last the shepherd David, quit his strife
with Saul, anointed king, besieged and vanquished   110
the Jebusites' proud citadel on Zion,
Jerusalem, the queen of all earth's cities,
which David then proclaimed his capital.
And David, beat of heart his love of God,
thought now of the Ark, prepared a place,
intending honor at his royal city,
and pitched a tent within his town to lodge
that holy guest, and bade the Levites and
their kinsfolk sanctify themselves to bring
the Ark into its tent with sacrifice   120
of ox and fatling, while the sacred charge
was borne by Levites' shoulders on stout staves,
their kin sang loud, played harp and psaltery
and crashed the cymbals. David, linen-clad
and girded with an ephod, midst the blare
of trumpet and cornet, the sounding out
of lyres and harps and cymbals, danced before
God's covenant with whirling steps and bounds,
and sang with vibrant singing brim of glee:

> The sea, let it roar   130
>   in its fulness!
> The fields, let them joy
>   in their burden!
> The trees of the wood,
>   let them sing Him,
> for joy of our Lord
>   Who is with us!

42

Lift up your heads, o gates,
  lift up your ancient doors!
The king of Glory enters!

    Who is this King of Glory?
      The Lord-God strong of hand,
    The Lord-God battle-mighty!

Lift up your heads, o gates,
  lift up your ancient doors!
The King of Glory enters!

    Who is this King of Glory?
      The Lord, the King of hosts!
    He is the King of Glory!

    Thus David sang in joy before the folk,   150
nor did it trouble him that Michal at
a window scorned her husband that he stripped
to leap as drunk with wine through love of God
though royal, unashamed before his servants;
he sang how presence of the Lord made honor
and majesty, His tabernacle beauty,
and vowed that he would be more unashamed
before the Lord, and viler in her eyes,
to render thanks to God for all His gifts.

    But he knew shame, shame the king should dwell   160
in noble house of cedar while the Ark
of God must dwell in tents—and would have built
a temple—purposed so indeed, but that
the Lord restrained through Nathan's lips, and said:
"Since I brought Israel from Egypt, when
have I once dwelt in cedar house, but walked
in tent and tabernacle? When have I
commanded any tribe of Israel
to build for Me a stately house of cedar?"

And David, God's beloved, never lapsed 170
in love or fear of God, obeyed the hest.
True that David, an inheritor
of our old stock, could fall to folly, most
because of love of women—though he was
the first to castigate his guilt as vice
and pray God's punishment be visited
on him alone, for David lived in love
(there never was more tender father loved
unworthy sons with such compassion, false
however proved or how rejecting love!). 180
And David held God's wishes firm in mind,
his faith, despite his acts, untarnished, pure.
Nor was his faith forgot when Absolom,
so richly loved, conspired to destroy
his loving father's life, and David fled
Jerusalem with all his faithful flock,
and Zadok and the Levites bore the Ark
beyond Brook Kidron in their flight; for David
demanded sternly: "Carry back God's Ark
into the city! If God wish to favor 190
His servant, He will know to bring me back;
if God take no delight in me, let Him
perform as Him seems good." Such perfect love,
such humbleness before the Lord King David
preserved, beloved of God. Nor failed the Lord
to justify his love, but brought him back.

In his last days the King at length convoked
his sons, his officers and ministers,
his captains, heroes, princes of the tribes,
and meekly spoke to them, for David's soul 200
still burned to honor God's great covenant
which lowly curtained long had dwelt in tents
through deserts and the wilderness, not yet
enshrined in noble house of thankfulness:
"I had in heart to build a house of rest

44

for the Ark of God, which houseless through the lands
has wandered for our sake, to build the Lord
a footstool for His feet. I made all ready
but God forestalled my hand and said,' Not you
shall build My house!'—for I have been a man 210
of war, have shed much blood in sight of God.
My son of peace, my Solomon, on you
depends the joyful sanction; you shall build
my house of God and prosper in that work.
Be strong and undismayed, for now behold:
I have prepared, you shall not want the means."
For David had forethought, "My son is young;
the house of God must be exceedingly
magnificent when built, inspiring fame
and glory through the lands." And David chose 220
the site the angel's sword had shown for altar,
the threshing-floor of Ornan, which as gift
good Ornan would have offered free, but David
would not accept until he paid to Ornan
in golden shekels fullest price for it.
And then he gathered store of brass and iron
for nails, and stone, and cedar-wood and olive,
and David did not cease preparing these
for Solomon, and he laid by much gold
and silver. Then he said to Solomon: 230
"You have a thousand thousand silver talents,
an hundred thousand more of gold, and bronze
and iron beyond their weighing, wood, and jewels,
and stone, and you may add—and masons, too,
and workers in abundance, skilled in every
of the cunning arts. Of gold, of silver, iron
and bronze there is no end. Arise, and do."
To four-and-twenty-thousand men he gave
to oversee the work, six thousand more
to judge and keep the records, four more thousands 240
to keep the doors, four thousands more to play
the instruments in praise of God, and said:

45

"Our Lord has granted rest to us; now He
shall rest in His Jerusalem forever.
No more the tabernacle need be carried
from place to place." Next he appointed who
must tend within God's house and who the courts
and chambers, purify the holy things,
who offer Sabbath sacrifice or on
new moons and days of feast, who governors,   250
who prophesy with lyres and harps and cymbals,
and who must teach the skill of sacred song.
The lots were cast for duties, great and small,
for teacher as for scholar.

                    Once again
King David spoke to Solomon his son:
"Solomon, in sight of Israel,
in hearing of the Lord, hear you my words:
take heed of God's commandments, learn to know
your Lord, to serve Him perfectly in heart
and willing mind, for He can search all hearts,   260
and He can trace to roots all thoughts. Seek Him
and you shall find Him; lose Him, He will cast
you off forever. Take you heed, for you
are chosen for this godly work. Be strong."
Thereafter David gave his son the plan
of porch, of houses, treasuries, the rooms
within, the upper chambers, mercy-seat,
the patterns of the courts and chambers round
about God's house, the ordered file of priests
and Levites and the craftsmen; gold by weight   270
for golden vessels, silver for the silver;
the weight of golden candlesticks, the lamps
of silver and of gold; the gold by weight
for tables of the shewbread, silver for
the silver tables; gold for forks and bowls
and cups, for golden basins, silver weight
for silver basins; gold refined to deck

the incense-altar; gold for chariot
of cherubim that spread their wings to shield
the Ark. Bronze there was for things of bronze, 280
and iron for iron, and wood for use of wood;
onyx and antimony, and stones
to set, the glistening and glittering,
stones divers-colored, precious past the measure;
and from the quarries marble mountain-massed.
Of David's proper goods, above the gift
for building, he bestowed three thousand talents
of gold that came from Indian Ophir, and
of silver freed of dross gave seven thousands
to overlay the Temple's walls without. 290
And David blessed the Lord and said, "O God,
sure, all the heavens and the earth are yours,
and yours our kingdom! Riches, honor, all
good comes from Thee. And who am I and what
my people that we gladly offer these
since all proceeds from you? We render back
your own, for we are the guests our fathers were,
and pass, our best of days a shadow; what
you lend we yield you! Keep your people's thoughts
on this: we cannot give, for all is yours!" 300
Then they assembled, blessed the Lord and burned
Him sacrifices of three thousand ewes
and rams and bullocks; with libations they
made feast that day before the Lord with joy.

These things occurred in David's latest years.
Then Solomon, his son, succeeded him.
From David he possessed capacities
beyond most men's; felicitous in singing,
he made five thousand songs; his lips poured grace,
quick sympathy and wisdom; and he spoke 310
three thousand saws replete with elegance
and wit; he was more beautiful than sons
of other men: locks black as raven's wing,

his visage ruddy, bright, attracting love,
his eyes like doves', a person (and the son
of such a father) framed for noblest deeds;
endowed beyond his fellows when he bowed
his heart in thanks for God's largesse. So gifted,
yet Solomon, uxorious, was not,
like David, perfect in his love for God.   320
The building of the Temple never granted
to David, God's beloved, fell to him,
King Solomon, most wise, most foolish king,
who could upraise his land to highest state
among the nations, and who sank to dark
impure idolatries of pagan gods
of abominable sodomitic rites,
Ashtoreth, cruel Molech, Chemosh, all
their practise vile. For it was Solomon,
who brought the Ark and what it held to rest   330
upon the mount where he caused build the Temple.
Upon that hill the patient Wanderer
reposed at last when Solomon encased
God's living Word in stone. Seven years
he was in building for the Lord—thirteen
he took to rear himself his royal palace!

When God had led his people out of Egypt
four hundred eighty years, the work began.
The King decreed no axe's clang, no thud
of hammer heard within the Temple's precincts,   340
the stone prepared in quarries—such respect
that time for modesty before the Lord
though shortly public scorn of purity
and private decency would show absurd
these strict observances! The walls within
were cedar, the floorings cypress, the cedar carved
with gourds and open flowers, that no stone
was seen. The inmost room enshrined the Ark—
its length, its width, its height each twenty cubits,—

all overlaid with rarest gold; there stood 350
two cherubim of olive wood, in height
ten cubits, touching wings above the Ark,
while to the other side the wing outstretched
five cubits to the wall; these two were also
thick overlaid with gold. The Temple's walls
were carved about with shape of cherub, palm,
and open flower, within and out, and all
was cased in gold, the doors and folding-doors,
the posts and beams. Ten stands of bronze stood by
whose border-frames on brazen chariot-wheels 360
portrayed the lions, oxen, cherubim
and wreaths; ten lavers, too, immense in bronze.
And so the work was done, the columns topped
with bowl-shaped capitals of network carved
in many hundred pomegranates. Bronze
and gold and stone and wood became God's house,
and Solomon exclaimed: "I built for Thee
a home to dwell, a settled place for Thy
abode forever!" Fourteen days a feast
was kept by king and all of Israel, 370
while Solomon made offering of many
an hundred thousand sheep and oxen praising
the Lord, and giving thanks.

        The years revolved
and Solomon to please his women built
for Chemosh a high place in the mountain,
for Molech, too; performed likewise to soothe
his other wives, burned incense, sacrifices
to honor stranger gods. David's dream
now fact in stone, the Ark was soon forgot; 380
wild folly then began to run a course.
The son of Solomon, King Rehoboam,
rejecting counsel of his elders, told
the people: "Solomon chastized with whips,
but I will chastize you with scorpions!"

And he erected poles on every hill,
beneath each tree high places, images,
and sacred pillars; men enacted there
the loathsome cults and fierce fertility
observances. Then came against them Shishaks,   390
the King of Egypt, plundering the treasures
of God's house. The nation split by now in two,
the northern prince, King Jeroboam, set
a golden calf in Dan and yet one more
in Bethel too and said: "Behold your gods,
deliverers from Egypt!" Under Ahab
in Israel vile Baal was worshipped next;
then Jezebel against the virtuous
brought lying witnesses and witch's wiles;
Jehoram, murderer of brothers, forced   400
the land to service of impiety;
Arabian and Philistine marauded
new plunder. Athaliah, infanticide,
converter of all Judah's sacred things
for use of Baal which David meant for God,
was slain by sword, and for a little space
the Southern Kingdom turned to God and broke
the sacrilegious altars, cleansed God's house—
but for a little space. While to the North,
in Israel, the upstart Jehu bowed   410
his neck to Shalmeneser, paying tribute.
Soon Syrian Hazael went up against
that land; its coward king despoiled God's house
and gave its gold in eager tribute pay.
Next Amaziah fell to pagan gods,
and Judah's Temple-hoard was plundered. There
the populace pursued unlawful rites
while King Uzziah added gates for God;
then Jotham added holy towers while
profane and still erect the poles stood honored.   420
In hopes to smooth Assyria, the traitor
King Ahaz robbed God's dwelling; he constructed

50

all corners of Jerusalem new altars
to his Damascan gods; he stole the bronze
devoted altar to Jehovah for
Damascan houses, cut the border-frames
and lavers, took the Sabbath covert out,
and offered his vile gods his sons in fire
as sacrifices burnt according to
their savage ways. Meanwhile the Northern Kingdom,   430
for long Assyria's prey, more than a third
of all the tribes already carried off,
by sword of Sargon was at last destroyed.
But David's town survived: had Judah eyes
the Lord gave ample testimony when
great Hezekiah brought his people back
to God! That noble king destroyed the bad
his father worked, restored the Temple's own,
replaced the pillage, and the Lord bestowed
full mercy on Jerusalem and wrought   440
Sennacherib destruction when the city
seemed surely lost before his horde. Once safe,
depraved Jerusalem again piled up
ingratitude. Manasseh reared anew
high places, altars, poles for Baal; in
the very courts of God's house deities
of hell discovered room; he set within
the Temple Asherah, Phoenician goddess,
large carved in wood; and witchcraft, augury
diverted him; and necromancers' wiles   450
and wizards' whims directing him, he drove
his son through flames, idolatrous; he shed
much blood of innocents, until the city
from one end to the other in his sins
had foundered. Amon, his weak son, contented
himself to trace that path his father cut,
until his men conspired death and stopped
his vicious days. For one-and-thirty years
was Judah blessed before the judgment came,

while Amon's son Josiah ruled with zeal   460
unequalled since King David lived. He spared
no evil standing, dispossessed both Baal
and Asherah, and sundered those foul houses
where sodomites participated in
their ruttish rituals and women wove
for Asherah her tunics; he pulled down
as well the satyrs' places near the gate,
and Molech's sites where many years the sons
and weeping daughters had endured perforce
the scorching flames. He reaved the Sun with crash   470
of bronze his chariots and brazen horses;
he razed that hill where Solomon revered
horned Ashtoreth and all those Moabite
and Ammonite abominations, smashed
the sacred pillars, poles, lewd palaces;
from Geba far as Beërsheba, yes,
in Topheth, Bethel, in Samaria,
he purged Jerusalem's environs of
profane ingratitude to right and left.
His son Jehoahaz ruled but three moons,   480
yet time Josiah's good to inquinate;
and Pharaoh took him prisoner, appointing
Jehoiakim as king, whose sufferance
it was to witness thankless Israel
for folly's long accumulated count
at last subpoenaed. Doom impending, he
blind blundered, studious to prolong the vice
his fathers flattered; first as Pharaoh's slave
he fell as prey, Nebuchadnezzar's next,
who brought him and his cowardly successors   490
to capture and to death in Babylon.
Though warned by Jeremiah, man of God,
those brutish kings, their tainted people, their
reprobate high-priests but mocked his warnings,
despised the pointing fingers of the seers
and labefied King David's Temple; until

a hostelry of crime, it was polluted;
until no remedy remained but that
there be an end of this mocking
anamorphosis of God's intent,   500
that it should crash to shards and dust
in broken dissolution. The Chaldee king
allowed Jerusalem no interim
of pity, no last hope. The butcher's sword
within the late-remembered sanctuary
slew young and old, strong men and pleading women,
the hale, the halt; Mount Zion saw her daughters,
deflowered by ravishers, then slain—her elders
buffeted with scorn, her princes hanged
by thumbs, saw all the Temple's treasures, gold
and silver, bronze and marble, pillars, bowls,   510
all pitchers, basins, cups which Solomon
had forged the Lord, all capitals and wreaths,
the bases, shovels, pots, the snuffers, forks,
and every sacred vessel, great and small,
seized by Nebuzaradan, Nebuchadnezzar's
high chief, who burned the house of God where God
had long been exiled, broke the city walls,
and flared in flames the royal palaces
and every house of note or worth. And now
depopulate and desert lay once proud   520
Jerusalem, the Holy City planned
by David, city now of blackened ruin
and broken stone, a home where only famine
could feast. To slavery in iron chains
were gone the pride of Judah in their strength,
the poorest only left behind to weep
and starve the centuries of evil done,
share bleak desolation with gnawing rat,
the tooth of jackal and the vulture's beak.

(Jerusalem Jerusalem! How lone   530
the city sits that was so full of living!

So proud a bride before, a widow now!
A princess once and now a fettered slave!
She weeps her bitterness alone at night,
the tears upon her cheeks, no comforter
of all her lovers left to dry them. Gone
her friends, betrayers all. The golden crown
is fallen from her head, her music stilled,
her dance has turned to mourning, in her heart
the dance of joy is stopped, the blood no more   540
can pulse, her eyes grow dim and die!

Jerusalem, do you recall God's love,
Your bridal love those days when Israel
was young still—how you followed Him through deserts,
through unsown lands, and barren fields and pits,
through drought and wilderness, through dark of vale
and dark of hill, and came to garden lands
to which He brought you, lands of ripening fruit?

He planted you a noble vine, your seed
the truest but you revert to rankest weed.   550
Jerusalem, Jerusalem, whose roots
were planted by God's Goodness, yet so fleet
to run your tendrils round the trunk of death!

Jerusalem, what sore offense did you
observe in Him that you should run from Him
You've followed things of nothing. You
forsook the fount of living water, carved
cracked cisterns holding blessings as a sieve!
Now call upon the gods you hewed yourself,

your worshipped gods of cruelty and hate,   560
let them arise and save you in your need!
Ah! you have played the harlot with too many,
with countless idle lovers. Where are they
with whom you have not lain? By wayside paths
you waited like the desert Arabian

for lovers, and you sought them in the stews
and drains, the abattoir and charnel-house,
abodes of blood and death; your harlot-brow
knew never blush at murdered innocence!
Jerusalem, Jerusalem, that stopped 570
your ears against the truth, that stoned the good
whom God had sent to utter it to you!

Jerusalem! You scorned the fallow ground,
and sowed among the thorns and rocks! Your sons
were circumcized, yet kept before the Lord
the foreskins of their hearts! The angels ranged
your streets and searched your squares, and had they found
one man who lived with justice, loved the truth,
but one, there could have been then pardon for you.
There was not one. The poor, the rich, the great, 580
the low, the wise, the foolish, visages
more hard than rock, alike said, "All is well."
Jerusalem, Jerusalem, that set
security in walled and pillared stone,
in sword and rampart, while you reckoned nothing
the blood of innocents which stained your streets!

Jerusalem! The end for this was war,
a pitiless destruction wakened by
your folly that held purity too cheap
and goodness foolish; hate and greed with which 590
you smothered love became as bellows' breath
to raging whirlwinds, mighty hurricanes
of fire laying waste your habitations,
that dried the waters from your wells, and parched
the land on which there falls no rain again!
The hind that calves in fields repels its young
because there is no grass, and on the heights
the wild-ass stands, eyes lustreless, and gasps
for air because the earth affords no green,
no green thing grows upon the earth, the wind 600
as from an oven drives the yellow sand

in rasping echoes through the cracks of stone
which heap the Temple Mountain, stones amassed
for God, and now illapsed the jackal's lair!
Jerusalem, Jerusalem! How lone
the widowed city sits, her ruined crags
the graves of desolation and despair!)

The exile was for three-score years and ten
in Babylon, and Zion's harps were hung
by stranger streams, their music silenced midst   610
the noise of conquerors' rejoicing. Then
vain dreams possessed the slumbering Israel,
rebuilding new the ruined Temple's glory
in shadows of their troubled sleeping; there
again the sanctuary's inmost gloom
where but the High Priest penetrated once
each year for solemn expiation; fume
of incense sweetly soaring from gold altar
in fervent vapor, sign of Israel's
accepted prayers; the ever-living light
the seven-branched candlestick would shed,
the symbol of the Ark's pure radiance.
And now the Ark—where was it? No man knew,
and no man since has known. That beacon of
the people to the Land of Promise, lost
forever, was (some say) in Babylon
destroyed by Nebuchadnezzar. The Temple would
again be built, but never more to house—
or slight!—celestial guest. The Land had cast
aside the Promise; rise or fall the walls,   630
Jerusalem the holy after this
would figure but a land among the lands
on charts of mankind's hopes!

       Before the sword
of Persian Cyrus fell Assyria
and Babylon and Lydia, and he,

a friend to Judah, bade who willed return
into Jerusalem, and start afresh
the building of the Temple on the mount.
Zerubbabel, and Ezra later, led   640
the eager thousands back, with what escaped
the Chaldee grasp of Temple's furniture,
and Cyrus granted all that yet remained.
But most of Israel did not return,
the poorest only; Trans-Euphrates well
contented more, and others through the lands
began their wanderings, until their throngs
were crowded on all seas and countries, where
they dwell offending with their lore and presence,
alone among their enemies; there dwelt,   650
acknowledging but one metropolis,
but one—not Rome, not Alexandria,
not Antioch—none but Jerusalem:
a nation scattered through the world, its heart
beat there.

        The second Temple, raised at length,
exceeded far in pomp King Solomon's,
a miracle of artifice, though housing
God's ruined covenant no more. With wealth
the city prospered; festal days the press
of pilgrims swelled the streets. How strange! The dream   670
of poet David, mortal-fleshed, who lived
but one allotted span of years (the space
a sigh consumes against the centuries
his heirs devoted to its sullying),
bequeathed Jerusalem the semblance of
a life, inspired a ritual complex
and subtle, reverenced wherever dwelt
self-exiled Israel, the dream itself—?
a word, its essence lost, its spirit dead!
A poet mocked as dreamer by his race,   680
his music scarcely heard amid the clink

57

of many million minted coins, his thought
disdained as too transparent for a world
of stone—when all his age (what's bought and sold,
what's smelled and tasted, grasped and fought, what's robbed
and plotted, wept, enjoyed, or worked or ruined)—
when all those bitter rages, vainest raptures
are gathered to the dust that was their fathers'—
his dream rejects to die, takes on new life,
and those unborn are fated to live lives   690
forever haunted by that dreamer's shadow,
and innerly though they despise his dream
must mold their buying, selling, tears and joy
in a design that imitates the form
though it may flee the dream's true hopes and substance.
Their dreamers' names were ever on the lips
of Sadducee and Pharisee and scribe—
if not of David, then of Abraham,
Elijah, Moses, Isaac, or Isaiah—
in David's name set snares and dug steep pitfalls   700
to trap the feet of them that hunted truth.
Jerusalem, the mountain-desert town,
disputed much upon the laws, and nursed
its holy thousand moles expert to scrape
the paths to nowhere, holy thousands who
were skilled to run on every crooked path
between the rocks and grooves, not daring once
the open road. The Sadducees took shelter
beneath Mosaic law, and where its shade
not lay disdained to see; professed dismay
that any man, irreverent, deny
their right to lay up golden treasures, eat
from golden platters (where had Moses these
prohibited?); deplored the foolish zeal
that would oppose the Roman conqueror,
who never meddled with days of feast and prayer.
The people, sure, could make but a confusion
of such patrician wisdom; let them not

58

decipher it! Enough if righteously
they live according to the law, their days
prolonged and blessed with many children, as
was promised them! The Pharisees, the pure,
the set-apart, the sons of men who lived
by sweat, enthusiasts of text and subtlest
commentary, old or new, were loath
to take of gold or silver for their lore,
and held it holy to do work of hands,
denounced the Sadducean thirst of wealth
and power, yet with pride were puffed that they
could twist the Holy Writ with tortured craft,   730
untangle Scripture thread by thread, re-tie it
in knotted fringes like the borders of
their garments; plumed themselves on prayer and fast,
on flagellations and on charities,
paraded holiness as on their arms
they wore phylacteries conspicuous.
No rite, no rule must be omitted; they
more loved to be forbidden than to do.
They held their brethren of the soil and trades
as fools too inexpert to follow maze   740
of controversy, or expound the sum
of paces one may walk on Sabbath. Soon
must come the Liberator to expel
the unclean Roman; when he comes a rule
shall be for every minute of the day,
and life will be an endless joy of sharp
dispute and closely reasoned argument
in which the mind will grow in strength as flesh
and spirit die.

    Some said in Bethany
a man of miracles sojourned this day,   750
descended, too, of David's line, and while
with clang and scratch the Temple's gates made way
for crowds of visitors that morn, were some

who up the other hill were streaming out
the town to visit Jesus, and to hear
and see what manner man could wake the dead.
Of them who came and spoke with him were few
could read their eyes' beholding or the words
pronounced; they climbed as to a market-place
not to a harvesting that Mount of Olives.   760
The piety of many urged them probe
if he whose death the Sanhedrin wished frame
indeed upon the Sabbath healed the sick
and raised the feeble; mingled in that crew
were mischief-forgers, self-appointed spies
athirst to fetch grave charges of blasphemy
to the high-priests. "It's said," the whispers ran,
"in synagogue on Sabbath he restored
a Galilean's withered arm."—"On yet
another he released a woman bent   770
in two by evil spirits."—"Sabbath day
last summer his disciples plucked and ate
the ripened corn in Galilean fields;
to pluck's to reap—which counts as labor. Ere
they ate, did they not rub to cleanse the chaff,
which differs how from grinding? Sabbath-scoffers,
who reap and grind to make a Sabbath bread!"
(But Jesus said: "The Sabbath's made for man,
not man made for the Sabbath.") Others told:
"Yes, in Samaria, near Gerizim
whose hated site would challenge as God's dwelling
Jerusalem's true Temple of the Lord,
he has not scrupled to call to his allegiance
Samaritans, our ancient foes." And some
inflated in their virtue spewed suspicion
on Jesus' holiness: "Has he with whores
not sat and dined, discoursed them tender words,
rebuking harshly pious scribes?" (What need
but by the sick of the physician's art?
And if a single sheep be gone astray   790

60

will not the shepherd leave the ninety-nine
and in the mountain seek the lost, which when
he finds will more rejoice him of that one
than of his five-score flock that did not wander?
What woman having ten denarii
if she should lose but one, will never light
a candle, sweep the house, and seek that one?
And when the coin's restored she calls her friends
and cries, "Rejoice with me for I have found
the piece I lost!" The angels joy in Heaven   800
when but one sinner can repent. Does not
the father kill the fatted calf when home
the prodigal returns back to his heart?)

Thus buzzed his enemies, not farther from
his teachings than his friends. For these, with mind
enchained to worldly hopes, could think of hope
of world-dominion solely. Hating Rome,
they thought the Master, David's scion, might seize
on David's throne, as had been prophesied,
and break their bonds to snatch the lordship of   810
the world, and crown Judea queen of earth,
beneath whose sway the Gentiles should be chained
as slaves. "It was foretold," some said, "that up
into a mountain we must go to hear
good tidings. Hence we've mounted to this height."
Such scraps of ancient saws affixed their dreams!
That God had long since ceased to call on Judah
to do His work, they had not noted; that
they were no longer chosen, they'd not seen!
Not through their walled labyrinths God's road!   820
Self-flattering, indigitating their
best Sabbath garb, they hinted they had conned
their part if Jesus were prepared to play
his role of Jewish Caesar, quoting Writ:
"Put on thy best of garments, captive Zion;"—
they cited tags: how Canaan must serve Shem,

as Noah told—how Balaam saw the Star
of Jacob's house and out of Israel
the sceptre which should smite on Moab's corners
and devastate all tumult's children, saying: 830
"Henceforth no more upon Jerusalem
uncircumcized, unclean, shall tread our foes!
For now is come a rod of Jesse's stem,
a branch shot from his roots! Now with the rod
of Heaven he'll strike the earth, and with his breath
shall slay the wicked heathen; for the Jews
he'll stand an ensign, and with him the day
of wrath shall break, and he shall smite their kings;
for he is sent the scourge in Zion's hand,
a lash to find out all our enemies!   840
His time of anger's here to heat them as
a fiery oven; his fire will devour,
shall swallow them! Yes, with an iron rod
he'll crush them; like a potter's vessel he
shall shatter them in pieces! He shall fill
with dead the places of the pagan lands!
The heathen shall be our inheritance,
the furthest parts of earth by him be ours.
Then let us therefore worship him lest he
enkindle wrath on us and we should die!"

                                                                850

For this was Balaam thrice delivered by
his faithful beast the seraph's sword, and thrice
who came to curse the chosen stayed to bless!
For this the shepherd singer's harp with song
had soared to thank the God he loved! For this
Isaiah touched the live coal with his lips,
extending God's salvation to the just—
for this he warned destruction lay in wait
and all that woe in Babylon, while greed
and gleam of gold usurped the light of God!   860

This way beset by enemies, self-deaf
to truth, this way misspelled by foolish friends,
now Jesus, sure his time at hand, began
an end of semination and delay;
if sacrifice alone could haste the tilth
of slag-souled Israel, God's chosen once,
he chose that husbandry. Wherefore, next morn
he bade of two disciples they convey
a foal, which seeking, found yoked to a post,
as soul of Israel tied fast to folly,   870
for their Deliverer they loosed of chain.
They decked their humble cloaks athwart the foal's
hard back, and Jesus sat on it. He then
descended down that stone-obstruent slope
which curved a road from the Mount of Olives to
Jerusalem. And as he went the people
spread clothes upon the path. Noon's gold lay bright
on vineyard, orchard, field, and tuft; mild breeze
that April Sunday fanned the palms' green fronds.
Of these a multitude of his disciples   880
cut each a branch beneath the cloudless skies
and scattered them before his calm advance;
but some with shouting waved the palm in hand;
first Peter, then the people, sang in joy:
"Hosanna! Blessed is our King who comes
in meekness, as it was foretold to us!
Hosanna to the son of David's line!"

At Bethphage the pomiferous where bloomed
fig-groves, when they came near the crofts, new crowds
of people from the land and town joined them.   890
And some entwined their hands in dance about
the silent Master, and before his way,
now clapping hands, now making earth and air
resound with mighty stamp of joyous feet:

Glory be to Thee, O Lord!
Thou the faithful will reward!
Glory be to Thee, O Word!
For Thy Grace our thanks be heard!
Glory Thine, O Holy One!
Do we sing in unison!   900
Glory to Thy Glory be!
Glory to Eternity!

We praise, Thee, O Father, we thank Thee, O Light,
Whose radiance lives and banishes night!
For we would be saved, and we would be loosed,
And we would be heard, from bondage seduced!

And we would be thought, and we would be seen,
And we would be hearkened, and we would be clean!

Grace dances; I dance.
Grace sings; I sing.

For grace I dance.
For grace I sing.

I fly not, but stay.
My place I would pray.
A temple I crave!
A lamp I would have!
My door wide to Thee!
Be Thine then to me!

Amidst this ferment, tranquil pivoting,
the little ass with measured gait and slow,   920
as conscious of the awful dignity
it bore, pursued in peace its stony path.
The Master pondering his private thoughts
appeared unhearing, brow serene in sun
like to a jewel of depthless light which flashes
innumerable rays around, itself

64

contained and pure, self-radiant and whole.
The nearer that they came Jerusalem,
the louder grew their shouts, more wild their dance.

One moment, though they did not mark, the foal,   930
restrained by Jesus' hand, forebore to move,
while Jesus viewed the city at his feet,
in sunlight yellow sand and stone, and wept.

(Jerusalem, Jerusalem, O you
who kill the prophets, stoning them that are
sent you! How often would this son of man
have gathered to him all your children as
a hen beneath her wings will gather chickens,
but you would not! Again and yet again
you made a mockery of man's best hopes,   940
a travesty of holiness, buffooned
the goodness and the love by which alone
the world can live! Yet once again it's yours
to hold the light before the peoples if
you choose—the last time such a choice is yours!
And you would not! And now your home shall fall
to desolation! Did you know but now,
this day at last, the things belonging to
your peace, the future hidden from your eyes!
Alas! The day soon comes upon you when   950
your enemies shall cast a trench about you,
encompass you, on every side keep you
shut in, shall lay you even with the ground,
your sons and daughters in you; fearful their
destruction, fearful and more lasting than
when Babylon came up against your walls!
They'll leave no stone upon another! They
shall send you forth to wander all the earth—
who did not know the time or him who came!)   999
(End of Book One)

65